ANIMALS UNDER THREAT
BLACK RHINO

IN DANGER OF EXTINCTION!

Richard Spilsbury

Heinemann
LIBRARY

www.heinemann.co.uk/library
Visit our website to find out more information about **Heinemann Library** books.

To order:
☎ Phone 44 (0) 1865 888066
▤ Send a fax to 44 (0) 1865 314091
▭ Visit the Heinemann Bookshop at www.heinemann.co.uk/library to browse our catalogue and order online.

First published in Great Britain by Heinemann Library, Halley Court, Jordan Hill, Oxford OX2 8EJ, part of Harcourt Education. Heinemann is a registered trademark of Harcourt Education Ltd.

Editorial: Emma Lynch, Jilly Attwood and Claire Throp
Design: Jo Hinton-Malivoire and Tokay, Bicester, UK (www.tokay.co.uk)
Picture Research: Rosie Garai and Liz Eddison
Production: Séverine Ribierre

Originated by Ambassador Litho Ltd
Printed in China by WKT Company Limited

ISBN 0 431 18889 0
08 07 06 05 04
10 9 8 7 6 5 4 3 2 1

British Library Cataloguing in Publication Data
Spilsbury, Richard
Black Rhino - (Animals under threat)
599.6'68
A full catalogue record for this book is available from the British Library.

Acknowledgements
The Publishers would like to thank the following for permission to reproduce photographs: Ardea pp. **14** (Ferrero-Labat), **7** (Ian Beames), **27** (Pat Morris), **23** (R.F. Porter); Corbis pp. **4** (Carl & Ann Purcell), **29** (Buddy Mays), **11** (FLPA/Terry Whittaker), **25**, **35** (Gallo Images/Anthony Bannister), **33** (Gallo Images/Martin Harvey), **16** (Peter Johnson), **10** (Robert Holmes), **40** (W. Perry Conway); Ecoscene p. **39** (Chinch Gryniewicz); FPLA pp. **8** (Eichhorn Zingel), **36** (F. Hartmann), **18** (Leonard Lee Rue), **5**, **12** (Martin Withers), **34** (Tony Hamblin); Getty Images p. **20** (Nicholas Parfitt); Images of Africa pp. **30**, **31**; Images of Africa p. **9** (David Keith Jones); NHPA pp. **21** (Jonathan & Angela Scott), **15**, **24** (Martin Harvey), **22** (Steve Robinson); OSF pp. **32** (Des & Jen Bartlett), **28** (Mike Powles), **38** (Paul Franklin); PA Photos pp. **26** (Michael Stephens), **43** (Michael Walter); Rhino Ark Kenya Charitable Trust p. **37**; Steve Bloom p. **19**; Tudor Photography p. **42**.

Cover photograph reproduced with permission of Corbis/Gallo Images/Martin Harvey.

The publishers would like to thank Dr Chris Tydeman, Environmental Consultant, for his assistance in the preparation of this book.

The author would like to thank Zoe Jewell for supplying the map reference for p17.

Contents

Words printed in the text in bold, **like this**, are explained in the Glossary.

The black rhino

A rhino – full name rhinoceros – is one of the biggest land **mammals** on Earth. Rhinos have an unmistakable body shape. Their most distinctive feature is a single horn or a pair of horns on top of their head. The long, curved head is connected to a massive body, which is covered in tough, mostly hairless skin. The body is supported on short legs.

The rhinoceros family

The rhinoceros **family** is **classified** within a large group of mammals often called the **ungulates**. Ungulates are hoofed mammals, which means they carry their weight on the tips of just one or two elongated, large toes. Tough hooves protect these toes. The other toes are much smaller. Horses have a single hard hoof, but rhinos have three leathery hooves. The central toe is the one that carries the weight. The other two help with getting a grip on slippery ground.

The rhinoceros family contains five **species**. Three of them – the Indian, Javan and Sumatran rhinos – live in parts of Asia. The remaining two live in Africa. These are the black and the white rhino. Each species looks slightly different. For example, black rhinos have two horns and fairly unfolded skin, whereas Indian rhinos have one horn and deeply folded skin that looks a bit like plates of armour.

These black rhinos are similar in shape to all other members of the rhinoceros family

Adult black rhinos have two horns on their head and their upper lip is pointed. Their front horns can measure up to 1.4 metres long, shorter than the longest white rhino horns.

The black rhino

The black rhino (*Diceros bicornis*) has two horns. Its skin is the least folded of any rhino species. **Bull** (male) black rhinos can grow over 3 metres long and weigh more than 1 tonne. **Cows** (females) are generally slightly smaller. Despite their size, black rhinos are agile and can run fast for short bursts, sometimes topping 45 kilometres per hour!

The black rhino is a critically **endangered** animal. This means it is at great risk of becoming **extinct**. By far the biggest reason for this is that people kill rhinos for their horns. This book discusses why and how they have become so endangered, and what is being done to save them before it is too late.

All in the mouth

The black rhino is not black and the white rhino is not white. So why the names? The difference is in the shape of their mouth. The white rhino has wide flat lips, which it uses for grazing on grass, whereas the black rhino's lips are pointed. When English people visiting Africa in the past first saw white rhinos they were described by **Afrikaners** as 'wijd'. This means wide, referring to the shape of the rhinos' mouth. However, they took the 'wijd' to mean white because that's how the Afrikaners pronounced it. The name stuck. Black rhinos are not really black, although they are often darker in colour than white rhinos. The main reason for the name is to distinguish them from the white!

Black rhino country

In the past, large numbers of black rhinos roamed freely over a vast area of Central, East and southern Africa. Today, there are far fewer black rhinos. Small populations live in limited patches of land scattered across this former area. Over 80 per cent of all black rhinos now live in the southern African countries of Namibia, Zimbabwe and South Africa.

Four rhino subspecies

A **species** is usually defined as a type of living thing that can **breed** successfully together to produce healthy offspring. Some species contain several different **subspecies**. Subspecies can also breed together, but are usually different in appearance or live in different places. Scientists divide black rhinos into four separate subspecies, each are living in a different part of Africa. The western black rhino lives in Cameroon, while the eastern black rhino lives mostly in Kenya. The south-western black rhino – or desert rhino – lives mostly in dry areas fringing deserts in Namibia, and the south-central black rhino lives mostly in South Africa and Zimbabwe.

Each subspecies looks slightly different. For example, the eastern subspecies has slender, curved horns and ridged, folded skin on its sides. The desert rhino is the largest subspecies, and has straighter horns than the others.

Black rhino –
Diceros bicornis

Historic and present distribution
- Current distribution
- Distribution in the past

▲ *Black rhinos were once widespread through half of Africa. Now they are only found in small parts of this former area.*

Like most black rhinos, these rhinos live in bushveld habitats.

A range of habitats

Black rhinos live in a range of **habitats**, which provide the resources, or useful things, they need to live such as food, water and shelter. Some black rhinos live in rocky desert habitats with few plants, while others live in rainforests on lower mountain slopes. However, most live in **bushveld** habitat.

Bushveld habitat is characterized by some coarse grass among scattered, dense areas of tough shrubs and trees such as wild fig and marula. These areas are called thickets. Thickets provide cover and shade for black rhinos and other bushveld animals. The branches of some of the trees and shrubs, such as acacias and camel thorn, are covered in sharp thorns that put off some animal **browsers**. In drier areas, water is extremely scarce. Plants that grow there, such as rock figs and euphorbias, have deep roots to reach underground water. They also have small, **succulent** leaves and fleshy stems that contain a store of water.

Black rhinos share this habitat with a wide variety of other animals, including large browsers such as elephant, kudu and giraffe. They sometimes overlap with white rhinos in grassier areas.

Climate

Bushveld typically forms in areas with a **tropical climate**. These areas have a hot, wet season and a cool, dry winter. Temperatures during the hottest times of day can reach 40 °C. Night-time temperatures are much lower, but rarely cold enough for any frost to form.

Black rhino populations

In the 1960s, scientists estimated there were as many as 100,000 black rhinos in Africa. In 2003, there are at most 3100. The population has fallen dramatically because of the demand for rhino horn.

The black rhino is already **extinct** in some areas. In others it is likely to be extinct very soon. Black rhino population counts for Cameroon, Malawi and Swaziland were ten or fewer in 2002. In a few places population estimates are much larger. In South Africa, for example, home of the commonest **subspecies**, the south-central black rhino, there are over 1000.

Counting black rhinos from the air, using light aircraft or hot-air balloons, is expensive and time-consuming.

Counting rhinos

Black rhinos are large, easily recognizable animals that should be quite easy to count. However, they often hide in thickets or other shade during the day. They are more active at dusk and at night, when it is cooler.

Scientists use several ways to estimate rhino populations. Some involve counting rhinos, either from the ground, by driving them out from cover, or from the air. There are several problems with these direct methods. They are disruptive for rhinos and other animals that live in the same **habitats**, and can be dangerous for the people counting them on the ground. Also, it is difficult to be certain you are not counting the same animals more than once.

Other ways of estimating

There are different ways of telling that black rhinos are present in an area, even if you cannot see them. Rhinos leave obvious signs such as piles of dung and **spoor**, or footprints. Although spoor can be used to recognize the presence and movements of particular individuals, it is time-consuming to find enough spoor over a wide area, and be able to tell them apart so that you can measure the population.

Most of these kinds of population estimates are based on a 'scaling-up' principle. First you find out how many rhinos live in a small area by carrying out lots of counts. Then you work out the total area of rhino habitat in the place you are studying. If there are, say, ten rhinos in 50 square kilometres, then in a total area of 500 square kilometres you assume there will be approximately 100 rhinos. This is scaling up.

Distance sampling is a counting method that uses the scaling-up principle. Scientists and helpers clear a series of random tracks in an area. Teams then walk along these tracks, at regular intervals, counting each rhino they see and measuring how far away it is using a device called a rangefinder. They assume there is a smaller chance of spotting rhinos further away. So, if one rhino is spotted 500 metres away, the distance sampling method assumes there are several other rhinos that were not spotted. A special computer program is used to estimate the population based on the data obtained.

▲ *From the ground, black rhinos are often tricky to spot. The signs they leave help people count them.*

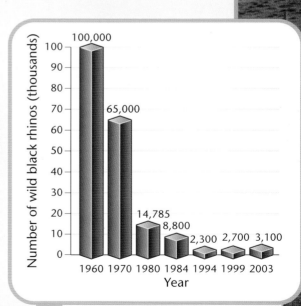

▲ *The black rhino population has dwindled to about 3 per cent of the 1960 estimate.*

The body of a rhino

Many people think rhinos look rather prehistoric, with their heavy, armoured bodies. The first rhinos that walked on Earth, around 50 million years ago, looked similar to the rhinos of today. A rhino's body has a range of special features, or adaptations, which it uses to help it survive in the hot, dry **habitats** where it lives.

Rhino horn

Rhinos use their horns as tools to help dig up or break off food. They also use them as weapons in fights. Unlike the horns of cows or sheep, which grow from the skull, rhino horns grow from the skin of the nose. They are made up of tightly intertwined strands of keratin (the material that makes up human hair) and gelatin (a jelly-like substance). Rhino horns are solid and heavy – the average black rhino adult carries around 4 kilograms of horn. The horns keep growing through a rhino's life, so older animals generally have longer horns. If they break or are cut off, rhino horns can regrow.

Barrel shape

Black rhinos are herbivores, which means they eat plants. The problem with eating plants is that the goodness in them is trapped within tough cells, and is therefore more difficult to release. This is why herbivores usually take longer to digest, or break down, their food than meat eaters.

A black rhino sometimes uses its horns to break off tree bark or snap off branches.

Black rhinos learn from an early age that mud helps them stay cool and keep insects off.

After a rhino chews some food it is partly digested by acids in its stomach. It then moves into the intestine. A large fold in the intestine contains **bacteria** that help to break open tough plant cells more quickly. The gases produced when this happens make the intestine swell up. The black rhino's body is shaped like a barrel because it has a massive stomach and a long intèstine, through which plant food moves slowly as it is digested.

Bare skin and mud

Black rhinos have very little hair on their skin, apart from their eyelashes and tufts in their ears and around the top of their tail. You might think this was to help them keep cool in hot habitats. However, unlike humans, rhinos cannot sweat to cool their skin. Instead, they avoid overheating by staying in the shade or by plastering themselves in mud at **mudwallows**, especially during the hottest part of the day. As the water in mud evaporates, it cools the skin. It also acts a bit like sunscreen cream.

Insect repellents

A thick coating of mud can also protect the skin from damage caused by insects. A rhino's skin is 2 centimetres thick, but it is sensitive and easily irritated by biting flies and skin **parasites** such as ticks. If there is no mud about, black rhinos often rely on **tickbirds**. These birds ride on rhinos, eating the skin parasites in the folds of their skin. Although tickbirds also irritate sensitive eyes and ears, and any wounds a rhino may have, they have the added bonus of calling if **predators** are approaching.

Black rhinos are **browsers**. This means they eat a mixture of leaves, branches, roots and bark from shrubs and trees. They eat over 200 different types of plant across Africa, but locally select fewer types. Their favourite food plants are spiny, for example whistling-thorn acacia. Black rhinos also like to eat euphorbia plants. These have a milky sap inside their stems, which can poison many other browsing species.

▲ The black rhino curls its prehensile lip around bits of food, and pulls them into its mouth.

Black rhinos are sometimes selective in which parts of plants they will eat. For example, they prefer giant fennel stems to the leaves. At other times they will eat the whole plant. What they eat depends partly on the season or where they live. As there is more new plant growth in the rainy season of the **bushveld**, rhinos may feed less at each plant. On the dry edges of the Namibian desert, **succulent** food plants are less common than in wetter areas, so desert rhinos are more likely to eat them completely. They will sometimes return to the same plant over several days.

A mini trunk

A black rhino's upper lip is pointed and prehensile, which means capable of gripping. It has no sharp front teeth to bite off food. It uses its tough lip, which is a bit like a mini elephant's trunk, to pull and prune. Inside its mouth, a bank of giant flat back teeth grind the food before it is swallowed.

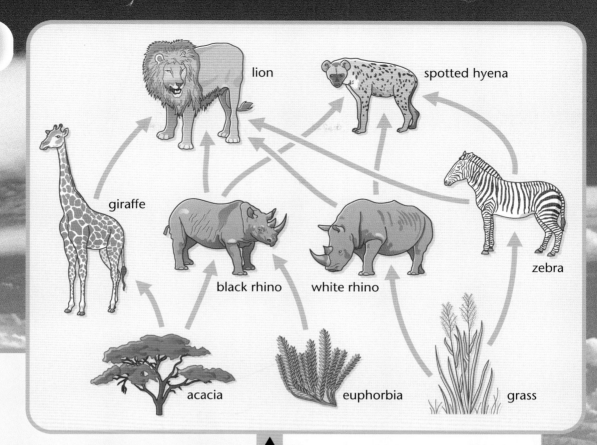

lion

spotted hyena

giraffe

black rhino

white rhino

zebra

acacia

euphorbia

grass

▲ The black rhino is just one part of an interconnecting food web involving many different African organisms.

Other needs

Plants provide rhinos with sugar for energy, protein for growth and repair, plus fat, fibre and other goodness. However, they do not provide everything rhinos need in certain habitats. Black rhinos need **mineral** salts. They get this from soil and soft rock. They use their feet and long horns to scrape up soil they can eat.

Black rhinos always live fairly close to a source of drinking water. They need water to wash down their dry, woody diet. Nevertheless, they can go for 3–4 days without water in dry conditions if they eat succulent plants. Although some may travel up to 25 kilometres each day to reach water-holes, most live within 3 kilometres of water. If there is not much surface water, black rhinos dig for water in sandy riverbeds.

Dung eating

Rhinos and some other **ungulates** eat dung to get the **bacteria** they need to help digest their food. Bacteria are tiny living things and a rhino's intestine is a warm, safe place with lots of food for them to live, grow and **breed**. This relationship is an example of symbiosis – when two living things rely on each other to survive. Baby rhinos are born without these bacteria, so the only way to get them is to eat the dung of other rhinos. Adult rhinos will also eat dung to top up their supplies of bacteria.

Communication and clans

Communication means exchanging information with others. Animals communicate in different ways. Black rhinos mostly use scents and sounds.

Black rhinos kick their hind legs backwards as they produce dung, scattering their scent around a midden.

Vision

Rhino eyesight is very poor. Rhinos can detect movement, but little detail of shape beyond around 20–30 metres. In the thickets of the bushveld, vision is a far less useful sense than hearing and smell.

Scent

Rhinos have a far more sensitive sense of smell than we do. They use it to pick up the scents of approaching **predators**, but also to know about other rhinos in the area. Rhinos can smell the difference between **bulls** and **cows**, and also between individual rhinos.

Middens (dung piles) have a vital place in black rhino life. Rhinos scatter middens throughout the area they live in. Each midden is visited by other rhinos, who smell it and poke it with their horns. Visitors also shuffle in the dung and then add to it. Bulls also spray urine on nearby bushes. Each midden, then, becomes a smelly message station. Any rhino that is in the area can tell who is around.

Clan members, especially cows, occasionally form larger groups to **browse**, to wallow in mud and to drink.

Sounds

Black rhinos are sometimes described as one of Africa's more 'talkative' animals. They make sounds ranging from deep bellows, growls and grunts to high squeals and screams. Different sounds have very specific meanings. For example, if the wind brings the scent of possible danger, they make warning snorts rather like explosive sneezes. If their calves are out of sight, cows call them back with a quiet mewing sound. Old bulls scream and snort when they challenge a rival to a fight.

Black rhinos have very good hearing. They use it to quickly recognize sounds made by other rhinos, but also the sounds of approaching predators. They can twist their trumpet-shaped ears in the direction of any sound, to listen to it more keenly while they carry on feeding. If they are still not sure what it is they will turn their head, look and smell the air.

Clans

Black rhinos do not live in family groups. Bull rhinos live rather solitary lives – they usually feed, travel and rest alone. Cows usually live only with their most recent calves. However, all the rhinos that live in one area form a community called a **clan**. Clan members do not have much to do with each other, but they accept each other's presence. They recognize each other by their smells, learnt and shared at middens. Clan members are not friendly towards any strange rhino that is detected. This is because strangers do not share their clan smell.

Black rhino home ranges

Each black rhino lives and moves through an area of **habitat** that provides the things it needs. This is called its **home range**. It is usually centred on a water-hole that only dries up in the driest years. The water is very important for drinking and for cooling down. The home range also contains enough plants for food and shelter. Black rhinos often shelter under large plants or overhanging rocks. Their regular movements to and from the water-holes create well-worn tracks.

Clan members usually have overlapping ranges, sometimes containing the same water-hole. Home ranges are much bigger in habitats where food and shelter are more widely scattered. For example, one reason desert rhinos – the south-western **subspecies** – have large ranges is because they have to travel to find shelter. On the hottest days of the year they climb from hot valley floors with little shade up to cooler, windy mountain ledges to avoid the extreme heat.

Territory

A **territory** is a part of a home range that a **bull** keeps other bulls out of when there is a female ready to **mate**. **Middens** warn other bulls not to trespass, but are also used to attract females. If an unknown male does trespass, the territory-owning bull usually attacks. He approaches making a screaming or groaning sound. If this does not warn off the intruder, the two rhinos may fight by clashing their horns. This is called jousting.

Black rhino horns are strong enough to puncture metal, but they rarely kill an opponent in a fight.

16

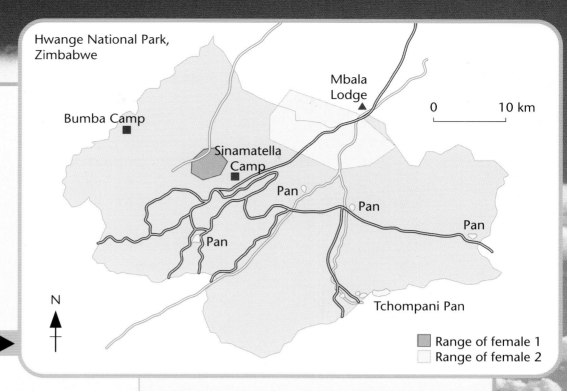

Hwange National Park, Zimbabwe

Bumba Camp

Mbala Lodge

Sinamatella Camp

Pan

Pan

Pan

Pan

Tchompani Pan

N

0   10 km

Range of female 1
Range of female 2

This map shows the home ranges of two black rhino cows in Zimbabwe. Pans are places where water collects in the rainy season.

Rank

Most encounters between bulls do not end up in a clash because the smaller, weaker rhino retreats. The winner may chase the other bull for up to 2 kilometres as it runs away. Afterwards the loser will avoid the winning bull's territory. Bull rhinos in a clan use close-up contests to work out rank. The higher-ranking rhino is the more regular winner of any fights, and more likely to mate with females in the clan.

Measuring home ranges

Scientists work out rhino ranges by recording where they move. It is difficult and dangerous to follow rhinos around in the **bushveld**, so scientists often use radio tracking. This is when a rhino is shot with a **tranquilizer** dart and fitted with a collar that gives off a radio signal. When the rhino moves off, a receiver tracks where it goes. There are several problems with radio-tracking. For example, it is expensive to buy equipment, and many collars either fall off or rub the skin underneath, causing infections.

Two rhino scientists, called Zoe Jewell and Sky Alibhai, began tracking black rhinos using their individually recognizable **spoor**. Local people had been tracking animals this way for generations. Jewell and Alibhai did it without this experience by loading images of different spoor on to a computer. Now whenever a track is found, it can be digitally photographed and the image matched up with the spoor using special software. The equipment is cheaper and training far simpler than it is for radio-tracking.

Courtship and breeding

Black rhino populations take a long time to increase. This is because rhinos **breed** very slowly. Few calves are born and they take a long time to become mature (able to breed themselves).

Courtship

Courtship is the first stage of breeding. This is when two adults establish whether they want to **mate** with each other. The first step is for the **cow** to enter a **bull's territory**. The bull then trails the cow at a distance so she gets used to his presence. She can smell and hear him. He also occasionally charges towards her but she turns towards him, threatens to attack and he backs away. Trailing like this can take up to six weeks.

Then the cow becomes ready to mate. The bull can tell she is ready because her smell changes. He pauses at places where she has urinated, and smells the air. He tastes the smell in an especially sensitive area in the roof of his mouth called the Jacobson's organ.

Breeding facts

Black rhinos can live for up to 35 years in the wild.

They become mature when they are about seven years old.

In adulthood, cows can give birth to one calf every three or four years.

This black bull is concentrating on the cow's smell to find out if she is ready to mate.

Newborn black rhino calves are on their feet, walking around, within ten minutes of birth.

Mating

Eventually the bull starts to edge closer, head lowered, swinging his horn from side to side, making puffing snorts. He sometimes adds dung to nearby **middens** and scatters it around with his horn. The cow sometimes chases him off once more or tries to leave his territory, but he usually blocks her retreat.

Eventually she trusts him enough to come closer still. She often makes a whistling noise to which the bull responds with small, stiff-legged steps of his front feet, while dragging his back feet. He often then rests his head on her side before they finally mate.

Pregnancy

Once they have mated, the bull leaves. He takes no part in looking after his baby. Usually he then searches for other females to mate with. Each female becomes ready to mate once every month. However, most become pregnant at a particular time of year, so that calves are born during the rainy season when food is plentiful.

A cow is pregnant for 15 or 16 months. During this time she becomes very grumpy and aggressively chases off most other rhinos that come close. She takes about ten minutes to give birth, which she does standing up. The baby falls onto the ground and she licks it clean.

Young black rhinos

Rhino calves drink large quantities of milk – a three-month-old calf may drink 20–30 litres each day.

Newborn black rhino calves are around 45 centimetres tall and weigh 40 kilograms, the size of a large dog. Their horns are around 1 centimetre high, and look like slight bumps on their snout. Although a calf is strong and can run within a few days of birth, this is the most vulnerable time in its life. It depends on its mother for food and protection.

A black rhino **cow's** milk is a complete food for its newborn calf. The milk is low in fat and high in energy and protein. Calves have no teeth when they are first born. These emerge when they are one or two months old. This is when calves start to **browse** on small amounts of plant food. However, it usually takes over two years before they are fully **weaned**.

Knowing the range

While her calf is still suckling, the cow stays in a specific part of her **home range**. During this time, her calf gets to know the area, too, including the appearance and location of food, water-holes and shelter. When the calf is weaned, the cow moves to a different part of her home range, leaving the calf to fend for itself.

Although the weaned calf may follow its mother, she will only let it stay with her for a while if she is not pregnant with a new calf. Then she will chase the older calf away. The older calf returns to live in the part of the home range where it was born. It stays there but may eventually enlarge its home range by moving into new areas of the **habitat**. For example, rhinos often move into areas where there is a lot of new plant growth brought on by early rains. Young adult rhinos, especially females, sometimes form small groups with other members of the same sex in their **clan**.

Protection

Before it is weaned, a black rhino calf stays near its mother for protection. The cow is experienced at smelling and hearing danger. If she senses a **predator** approaching, sometimes prompted by warning calls from **tickbirds**, she often moves upwind of the danger before attacking by charging. If the calf senses danger it squeals to alert its mother, who moves closer.

Predators

The most dangerous natural predators of black rhino calves are lions and spotted hyenas. Both hunt in groups. Although individually they are no match for a rhino cow, together several can distract her while others bring down her calf. These predators also occasionally target old, weak or sick adult rhinos. Rarely, elephants attack and kill adult rhinos in disputes over the use of **mudwallows**.

Black rhino calves always follow their mother when running. White rhino mothers always follow their calf!

Poaching

The dangers black rhinos face from natural **predators** are nothing compared with the dangers they face from people. **Poaching** is illegal hunting. Poachers are people who kill rhinos for their valuable horns.

Poachers often catch black rhinos in wire traps, or snares. They hide the snares on the rhino tracks to and from the water-holes on the **home range**. Death in a snare is slow and painful. Poachers also use quicker methods to kill rhinos such as machine guns. They cut the horns off dead rhinos using machetes, or even chainsaws.

Hunting in the past

The motive for killing rhinos has changed over time. Thousands of years ago, rhinos were killed for meat and for their thick hide, but also because they were dangerous. Rhinos remained plentiful until the early 19th century, when an estimated 1 million lived in Africa. In the 1850s, European explorers began to hunt rhinos for sport, using powerful guns, to prove they could kill a large wild animal. They took the horns to show off their skills. People soon realized they could make money by selling horns. By 1880 traders had begun to hire local hunters to collect horns of any size. Until the early 20th century, hunting rhinos was legal. As rhino populations began to fall drastically, more and more countries made hunting illegal.

▲ *Rhinos are often killed just for their horn, the rest of their body is left untouched.*

Rhino horn handles are traditionally prized in Yemen because they are rare. Polishing and carving reveals intricate fine lines in the horn.

Poaching facts

Between 1970 and 1987, over 80 per cent of all the world's rhinos disappeared.

In 1960, rhino horn cost £15 a kilogram. Today it costs up to £15,000 a kilogram, which is more than the price of a kilogram of pure gold.

Why do people want rhino horns?

People today want rhino horns for two main reasons. Both are based on cultural traditions. In Yemen and Oman, in the Middle East, there is a ceremony marking the time when boys come of age, or become men. At the ceremony they are presented with a ceremonial dagger called a **jambiya**, with a carved horn handle. Before the 1970s, only the richest people could afford the best jambiya handles, made of rhino horn. Most handles were made of cheaper horn such as water buffalo horn. During the 1970s and 1980s many Yemeni and Omani people became rich working in the oilfields of Saudi Arabia. More people wanted the best handles to show off their newfound wealth, so rhino poaching increased dramatically across Africa.

The biggest demand for rhino horn comes from South Asian countries such as China, Taiwan and India. Here it is a prized ingredient in traditional medicines. Horn is shaved or powdered and boiled up to make a potion that is claimed to have various powers such as treating fevers. Like jambiyas, the demand for expensive rhino-horn medicines has increased as people have become richer.

Dealing with poaching

People have tried to stop the **poaching** of black rhinos in several ways. One way is to make sure that laws preventing poaching are enforced. This is usually far more difficult than making the laws in the first place. A second way is to remove the rhinos' horns so poachers do not target them. A third way is to encourage people to use alternatives to rhino horn, by updating their traditions.

Enforcing

Black rhinos are protected animals in all countries where they live. This means it is against the law to kill a rhino and sell its horn. If poachers are caught they face punishments such as fines and imprisonment.

However, many people are prepared to take the risk. To a poor poacher in a poor country, even a small proportion of the price paid for rhino horn would be worth a risk. But the risk is actually not that big – the wilderness areas in Africa are huge and there are few wildlife **wardens** to catch poachers. The fines are often small. A poacher in Kenya is fined around £5 if they are caught.

Populations of black rhinos in several countries are protected with armed guards day and night, to deter poachers. The problem is that poachers are equally well equipped and can hurt and even kill the guards.

It is expensive to employ and equip wardens to stop rhino poachers.

*Dehorning was successful in slowing the poaching of the south-western **subspecies** in Namibia in the 1990s.*

Dehorning

Another way to stop poaching is to cut off the rhinos' horns without harming the animals. To do this, vets shoot the rhinos with **tranquilizer** darts to put them to sleep for a while. The horns are then cut off. Although horns are important to rhinos, in feeding, fighting and dung scattering, they can survive without them.

One of the problems of dehorning is that it is expensive to employ vets to do the job. It is not a one-off expense either – dehorning has to be repeated every few years as the horns regrow (at about 7 centimetres per year).

Rhino horn alternatives

Traditions are important to different cultures of people, but sometimes they need to be changed because they are not appropriate today. For example, while it is a tradition to have horn **jambiya** handles, many people believe they should not be made from the horns of **endangered** rhinos.

Although some traditional medicines are effective, some are not. Many scientists question the properties claimed for rhino-horn medicines, which were first used when rhinos were more plentiful. Their studies suggest, for example, that aspirin reduces fever far more effectively than rhino horn. Natural fever remedies and jambiya handles can both be made from the horn of water buffalo. Water buffalo are domesticated wild buffalo kept by millions of farmers throughout Asia. Their horns are readily available.

Conflict between black rhinos and people

Black rhino horns **poached** in African countries are eventually made into traditional medicines and **jambiyas** in countries in Asia and the Middle East. But how does the horn get there?

Trade routes

Today most black rhino poaching happens in northern Zimbabwe. Poachers generally cross from Zambia, to the north of Zimbabwe, at night. Although armed **wardens** monitor their movements and often stop the poachers, many will still get past and kill any rhino they find.

The rhino horn is then **smuggled** to Yemen by different routes. Sometimes smugglers transport it in small boats from east African ports, such as Mombasa, to Aden. Sometimes they fly to Yemen from Somalia or Sudan. However, smugglers often change their routes at short notice to avoid being caught.

Customs officers at national borders try to stop smugglers. They search luggage and cargo transported in boats and planes for concealed rhino horns, but it is difficult to stop smuggling. For example, wars in the region have meant that many **refugees** move across borders to escape trouble. Smugglers sometimes pay refugees to move the horn for them, or pay customs officers to ignore their activities.

These are rhino horns seized by customs officers in London in 1996.

Most governments are trying to stop the use of rhino horns in traditional medicine, but in some places their efforts are not working.

Working together

Demand for rhino horn can be reduced if countries work together to stop international trade. In 1975 the Convention on International Trade in Endangered Species in Wild Fauna and Flora (CITES, pronounced 'sightease') was formed. This is an agreement now signed by over 160 nations to regulate trade in **endangered** animals, including black rhinos, alive or dead.

CITES has been effective where member countries have enforced the laws. When Japan joined, the flourishing trade in imported rhino traditional medicine products dropped from 800 kilograms a year to zero. However, trade is not controlled carefully enough by some members, and is not controlled at all in non-member countries. When Sudan joined CITES, for example, smugglers simply found another air route to transport rhino horns.

Stockpiles of horns

In 1981 China joined CITES. However, it continues to allow unregulated trade in rhino horn. It claims the horn being traded comes from stockpiles of horn it collected before it joined, which can be legally traded. The problem is that newly poached horn is smuggled into stockpiles and then traded. Although changes in CITES agreements have demanded that member countries register their horn stockpiles, China remains the world's largest importer of rhino horn. So far, over 10 tonnes of rhino horn has been registered by CITES members – equivalent to 4000 dead rhinos, or more than the entire population of wild black rhinos.

Destroying black rhino habitats

▲ *This area of rhino habitat is being cleared to plant crops.*

The number of people on Earth is increasing rapidly. For example, in 1960 the population of Zimbabwe was less than 4 million, but in 2003 it was more than three times bigger, at over 14 million. More people need more land to live and work on, and more food to eat. This inevitably means natural habitats are destroyed resulting in a fall in many wildlife populations.

The need to cut down trees and other plants for firewood, and to provide grazing land and food for livestock are part of habitat destruction in the areas of Africa where black rhinos live. Cattle also destroy habitat by grazing and trampling plants, and by exposing and compacting the soil, so it gets worn away.

However, habitats are also destroyed when people clear land to build factories and dams, and dig mines. Local people may feel positive about these changes because new jobs may be created and they can reduce their dependence on aid from other countries. However, when land is cleared it not only destroys the habitat, it can affect the area in other ways. For example, mining for metal ores often generates a lot of poisonous waste that can pollute rivers and land.

▲ An isolated black rhino population may suffer from inbreeding.

Fragmentation

Some areas of black rhino habitat are isolated fragments of an area that was once larger. Fragmentation happens when people build roads, fences and farms that stop animals moving between the fragments.

Small areas can support fewer rhinos, because there is less food, water and shade. There is also less space for rhinos to establish **home ranges**. **Bulls** may fight more often over the **cows** that are ready to **breed** if their ranges are smaller or overlapping. When rhinos in an isolated population breed just with each other over several generations, it can also result in **inbreeding**. This is when a rhino population becomes weaker or less able to survive changes because they have very similar **genes**.

Ecosystems

Poaching rhinos also causes habitat change. Black rhinos are just one part of the **bushveld ecosystem**. An ecosystem is all the living and non-living things in an area and their relationships with each other. One small change in an ecosystem can affect many other parts of it. When many black rhinos in an area are poached, the number of shrubs there increases because there are no rhinos to eat them. When shrub thickets spread over grassy areas, there is less grass for grazers, such as zebras, to eat. They move away or starve, which means in turn there is less **prey** for the **predators** in the ecosystem.

Saving black rhino habitats

National parks

The first national parks in Africa were established in the 1920s. People who lived on the land were often moved off. For example, the Maasai people were shifted off the Serengeti National Park by the Tanzanian government. This changed their traditional way of life, as it excluded them from areas where they moved around in search of food at different times of year.

To preserve the **habitat** of **endangered** wildlife and to exclude **poachers**, **conservation** workers create protected areas. In general, the larger the area that is protected, the more wildlife **species** it can support. However, large reserves are difficult to set up and maintain. It may be expensive to buy the land. It will certainly be expensive to employ enough **wardens** and rangers and to equip them with, for example, vehicles, weapons and uniforms.

Although smaller reserves protect fewer animals and smaller areas of habitat, they are cheaper to run and can be protected more effectively. Wildlife outside the area is not protected.

Types of protected areas

Protected areas come in different sizes and types and are set up by different groups. National parks and reserves are generally set up by governments to protect a wide range of wildlife in a large area of habitat. Conservation areas, **sanctuaries** and intensive protection areas are usually dedicated to conserving a particular species, or special habitat, and are operated by **non-governmental organizations (NGOs)**.

Almost all wild black rhinos live in protected areas.

30

The cost of protecting rhinos

There is a conservation plan for the western black rhino **subspecies** in Cameroon, to establish a small sanctuary with a population of at least 50 animals by 2050. The sanctuary will be heavily patrolled by armed guards to protect the rhinos from poachers. Estimates for the cost of the project include £140,000 for finding, identifying and protecting five unrelated rhinos for up to two years while the sanctuary is being built, and £1.4 million to build it.

When elephants decide to eat crops, there is little that African farmers can do to prevent damage.

Boundary disputes

When a protected area is established, people outside its boundaries sometimes feel angry and resentful. They are kept off land where they once collected wood and water and hunted food. People living on the edge of the protected area are also threatened by the protected wildlife. For example, elephants may trample their crops. Although black rhinos do not eat local people's crops – they remain on fixed **home ranges** with regular feeding routes and particular food plants – they are often protected in the same areas as elephants.

These problems cause more tension between people and animals. This may make local people more likely to kill the animals, to eat, sell or to help poachers. It is important to remember that what most people in developed countries think of as a rare animal, may be just another meal to local people.

Translocating black rhinos

Zoos and wildlife parks

Zoos and wildlife parks keep rhinos in captivity. In the past, rhinos were collected from the wild, but today rhinos are translocated from sanctuaries and ranches, or bred in the zoo. Captive rhinos are swapped between different zoos in different countries to **breed** as part of a breeding programme. This programme ensures that related rhinos do not breed, thus avoiding **inbreeding**.

People who run captive animal breeding programmes hope they can produce animals that can eventually be reintroduced into the wild. This is difficult for many reasons. Rhinos bred in captivity cannot learn how to avoid **predators**, find food or establish **home ranges**.

In some parts of Africa there are areas of good rhino **habitat**, but few, if any, rhinos living there. Other areas have plenty of wild rhino but are threatened by **poachers** or habitat destruction. Both problems can be solved by **translocation**, moving a wild animal from one place to another more suitable place to live.

Translocation of rhinos is not easy. Suitable animals are **tranquilized** and carefully moved using crane-mounted slings and lorries. This is a very complex operation, as rhinos can damage themselves by charging into unfamiliar objects when they wake up somewhere strange. Rhinos are slow to get used to new areas. They may eat unfamiliar plants that are poisonous to them, or stray over dangerous inclines. Their digestive systems are also sensitive to the disturbance caused by being transported. Many become ill on the journey, however well they are cared for.

► This black rhino has been translocated to a new habitat in Namibia.

Black rhino keepers bottle-feed orphans on special formula milk.

Rhino sanctuaries and ranches

Rhino **sanctuaries** and ranches are small, protected areas that are fenced off and guarded within larger protected areas. They encourage wild rhino breeding and rhinos are translocated from other ranches, to enlarge the existing population. Eventually, when the population has grown through breeding, some of the rhinos are then translocated to restock other areas. One of the most famous ranches, Solio, contains one fifth of all the black rhinos in Kenya.

Ranches also offer specialized care for orphan rhinos, left alone when their mothers are poached. Orphans miss out on learning from their mothers. The David Sheldrick Trust in Kenya has developed ways of successfully moving orphans reared on ranches back into the wild. The techniques the Trust uses, based on behaviour in the wild, have also been useful in caring for rhinos in zoos and wildlife parks.

Orphan calf care

These are some of the techniques rhino ranches use to raise orphan black rhino calves:

- The calf becomes familiar with several keepers so it is not reliant on just one.
- The calf is protected at night for the first three years in a stable, with articles of the keepers' clothing as a comforter.
- The calf is led around **middens** so it learns about the scents of other rhinos, and allowed to eat dung, to build up its intestine **bacteria**.
- The calf is encouraged to use a **mudwallow**, especially in hot weather.

Conservation efforts

It is not easy to justify spending money to save rhinos when local people are living in poverty.

The SADC rhino programme

The Southern African Development Community (SADC) is a partnership of southern African countries, where over 80 per cent of all black rhinos live. They run a Regional Programme for Rhino Conservation. The programme is coordinated by African government departments from each country such as the Ministry of Environment and Tourism in Namibia. They are helped by scientists specializing in rhino conservation, from organizations, such as IUCN and WWF, and by many local conservation workers who have detailed knowledge of specific areas of rhino habitat.

Most countries in Africa where black rhinos live are home to large numbers of poor people. These countries can barely afford the food and medicines their people need, let alone fund wildlife **conservation**.

In spite of this there are many expert and committed African people working to save black rhinos. Their conservation projects need money and expert help or equipment to set up and to keep going. They rely on help from national and local government, but also from international **aid**. Some international aid comes from other governments, but some comes from **NGOs**, including charities. Whether local, national or international, most raise money for conservation by donations from the public or businesses. Many rely on the work of **volunteers**.

How endangered?

Conservation specialists grade endangered animals into different categories depending on how much protection they need. All rhino species are ranked **CITES** Appendix 1, which means they are at risk of **extinction** within five years, and any trade in rhinos is illegal. IUCN produces a Red List with eight categories. The most threatened, like the black rhino, are called critically endangered.

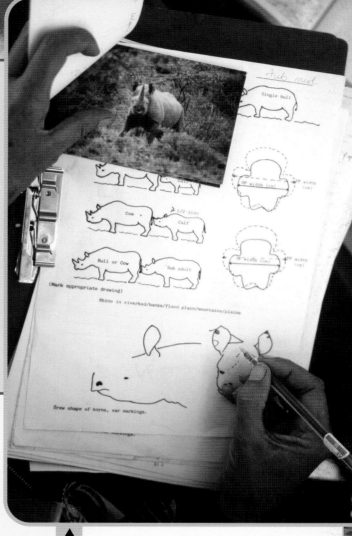

People sometimes pay to go on holidays where they work on conservation projects. This holidaymaker is using charts to recognize an individual black rhino for a population study.

Conservation projects

Black rhino conservation ranges from preventing **poaching** and **smuggling**, to learning more about rhino **habitat**, behaviour and population. Conservation groups usually concentrate fundraising on specific projects. They raise funds by, for example, advertising in the press or **campaigning** on the streets.

WWF is a massive international charity founded in 1961. Annually it spends around £100 million on conservation, most of it given as donations. It has several ongoing projects helping black rhinos. WWF describes black rhinos as a flagship **species**, an **endangered** species that inspires conservation not just of rhinos, but also of other less well-known creatures that live in their habitats. One project is a collaboration with TRAFFIC to build an international computer database of records of rhino horn captured by **customs** officers. The aim is to share information about the quantities of horn smuggled and the trade routes used. In other black rhino projects, WWF is training rangers in Namibia and providing technical expertise for private **sanctuaries** in Kenya and South Africa.

Aberdare National Park, Kenya

The government of Kenya, working with the charity Rhino Ark, is hoping to set up a new black rhino sanctuary. The plan is to establish the **sanctuary** in the mountainous part of the Aberdare National Park, a few hours' drive north of Nairobi in Kenya.

Background

In 1970 there were an estimated 20,000 black rhinos in Kenya, but now there are only around 400. The Kenyan government accepted that it failed to protect its rhinos from **poachers** in the mid 1980s. It decided to establish high-security, fenced and guarded sanctuaries. The sanctuaries were stocked with rhinos from ranches and scattered individuals **translocated** from other areas. Rhino numbers have increased in Lake Nakuru and Tsavo West sanctuaries, but more rhino **habitat** is needed.

Why Aberdare?

Aberdare is an area of uninhabited forest, scrub and thicket, ideal black rhino habitat. It contains highlands where rhinos will be able to stay but also encounter fewer ticks (insect pests), which can sometimes carry diseases. The area also supports a range of other wildlife such as the rare forest hog, elephant, leopard and bongo.

Aberdare has lots of water, which is ideal for rhinos but also for people. Its rivers supply local people and the growing population of Nairobi. Aberdare water will also be used in hydroelectric schemes to generate electricity. The electricity will not only benefit local people living around the park, but also power electric fences being built to keep poachers out and animals in.

This is just a small section of the Aberdare sanctuary fence already put up.

The 2002 Rhino Charge in Kenya raised over £200,000 for fencing the Aberdare sanctuary. Children help to raise money too, by taking part in the Hog Charge.

Fencing

As wildlife habitat shrinks and people move on to cleared land, they encounter wild animals more and more. Fencing can have great benefits for animals. It protects their habitat from further destruction. It can also have benefits for local communities, by stopping wildlife damaging their crops and killing their livestock. **Wardens** at gates in the fence will allow some access to the sanctuary to collect firewood. If any crop damage does occur, the sanctuary plans to pay for it.

Fence facts

The Aberdare sanctuary requires 380 kilometres of electric fence.

Clearing land and putting up electric fencing costs over £12,000 per kilometre.

At present rates, the fencing will not be finished until 2015.

Fundraising

Rhino Ark was set up in 1987 to help the Kenyan Wildlife Service pay for the building of this sanctuary. Funds are raised in many ways, such as the Hog Charge – a mountain bike event that children pay to enter and encourage sponsorship – and the sale of prints of a painting of an Aberdare water-hole. The biggest money raisers are the annual Rhino Charges, offroad races in 4x4 vehicles over tricky terrain. These take place in the Aberdares and in the UK.

Rhino Ark has also received invaluable voluntary help. In 1996 the British Army's Operation Crabapple built the main guard post. The Kenyan Army is to clear 40 kilometres of land so that fencing can be put up.

Black rhino tourism

A dead rhino is worth up to £25,000, but a living rhino is worth up to £250,000 a year as a tourist attraction.

Hunting as conservation?

Some southern African countries with large, stable rhino populations argue that a small amount of legal hunting could help rhinos. Money raised from selling expensive hunting licences would benefit protected areas and local communities. The idea has been successful in the conservation of white rhinos. One national park in Bophuthatswana raises almost enough money to keep it running, by selling ten hunting licences a year, at £6000 each. However, all rhinos are slow to **breed**, and without careful control of how many are hunted, populations will fall.

Large, impressive **endangered** animals, such as the black rhino, are a great attraction for tourists. Visitors pay money when they take safaris or visit protected areas, for example by hiring guides or paying entrance fees. Some of this money goes towards **conservation** projects and the upkeep of protected areas. Some of it also benefits local communities, especially if they are involved in running tourist facilities.

The pros and cons of tourism

Tourism has to be carefully managed. Although it brings in money and raises interest in conserving endangered animals, it can also cause problems. Too many people can scare away wildlife and affect the **habitat** it lives in, for example by wearing away the land. Safari vehicles and tourist hotels can also increase pollution, with sewage and litter.

Local involvement

Tourism sometimes does not benefit local people living near black rhinos. Sometimes money from tourism just goes to the owners of the land that rhinos live on, and to hotel owners or safari tour operators based in other places. Most Africans are too poor to own land or tourism companies. However, if communities of local people get some regular income from rhino tourism, they will help look after rhinos and their habitat. Rhinos will be worth more to them alive, by raising regular income from tourism, than dead, as a one-off **poaching** payment. Locals become involved in tourism in different ways. They can use their detailed knowledge of wildlife and local habitats, to work as guides and rangers for tourists.

Governments can support local tourism by taxing non-local hotel owners and tourist operators, and by not charging rent on land used for local tourism. Communities encourage visitors by managing campsites, craft centres and traditional villages. They share out much of the money raised within the community.

CAMPFIRE

Communal Areas Management Programme for Indigenous Resources (CAMPFIRE) is an organization in Zimbabwe that promotes community-based wildlife management. Each village in the organization has a wildlife committee, which monitors wildlife populations, works to prevent poaching and educates local people about looking after their environment. It also helps to sort out local problems. For example, the committee pays people for crop damage or injuries caused by wildlife.

A local school class visiting Anna Merz's rhino sanctuary in Kenya.

The future for black rhinos

There is an enormous amount of effort being put into black rhino **conservation**, by many people. Even so, many populations of black rhinos are in deep trouble. The two keys to the future for all black rhinos are changing trade and changing attitudes.

Changing trade

The international trade ban on rhinos has been a success. Without it, all five **species** of rhino on Earth would certainly now be **extinct**. However, the people who want to profit from selling rhino horn are very determined, and the remaining rhinos are gradually disappearing. Although the legal trade of rhino within most countries is now controlled, **smuggling** continues to thrive. This pushes up prices and makes more people want to smuggle. According to Esmond Bradley Martin, the WWF expert on the rhino trade: 'More rhino products are available in Bangkok than any other South-East Asian city.' This is despite Thailand being a member of CITES.

More money and effort needs to be spent on enforcing rhino trade laws within and between countries. But this is easier said than done. For example, in Yemen around half of all goods for sale are smuggled into the country, so it is even more difficult to trace rhino products.

Changing attitudes

One of the biggest obstacles to saving black rhinos is people's attitudes. For example, traditional medicines containing rhino horn have been used for thousands of years. People who use and sell them are not willing to change. Conservation organizations also need to tread carefully when trying to change people's attitudes, because of the need to respect the ideas and values of different cultures.

A conservation success story

White rhinos are also endangered, but there are far more of them than black rhinos. In 1885 there were just 50 – they were almost extinct. Today there are over 11,000. This was achieved by **translocating** rhinos into fenced private protected areas, and eventually moving them to other suitable protected areas of **habitat**.

Many experts predict that black rhinos could be totally extinct by about 2020.

The greatest challenge is to help more people in Africa understand that black rhinos are worth more to them alive, through tourism and conservation in which they are actively involved, than dead. As one Namibian put it, 'We used to get food and money from shooting animals, and now we get it from people coming to look at them. It's better that way.' This has proved successful in Namibia, where the population of black rhinos increased from 583 in 1994 to 893 in 2001.

How can you help?

If you are sitting in a school reading about black rhinos and the big problems they face such as **poaching**, **smuggling** and **habitat** destruction, it may feel frustrating. How could you possibly help save black rhinos from these problems? Well, the answer is to speak your mind – individual views do count. The people who make laws around the world listen to what individuals just like you have to say about how well they are protecting black rhinos.

Know more

The best first step is to know as much as you can about rhinos and the problems they face. Then you will be better able to tell people how you feel. You can learn more about rhinos in books and videos from your local or school library. You may be able to visit a museum, zoo or wildlife park near where you live. You may even have the opportunity to visit a protected area in Africa where wild rhinos live. Once you know more, tell other people – your family, your classmates, your neighbours – about the issues.

Go to the zoo

Zoos and wildlife parks around the world are important in spreading the word about rhinos. They offer a great opportunity to get close to rhinos and learn more about their lives. They are also an important part of rhino conservation, through their involvement in international **breeding** programmes and their fundraising for conservation organizations.

Learn about black rhinos wherever you can, from TV programmes and encyclopaedias to museums.

Spread the word

Now you know your stuff, get writing. There are lots of different rhino issues to focus on. Perhaps you would like shops to stop selling traditional medicines containing rhino horn, or feel that **jambiyas** should never be made of rhino horn. You might like to support a particular **conservation** project such as fencing part of a **national park** for the protection of rhinos.

Write a letter about how you feel and send it to a local or national newspaper, or direct to your government or state representative. Some conservation organizations have details on their websites on how to word a letter effectively, and who to send it to. Instead of writing your own letter you could add your signature to a petition – a letter about a particular cause you agree with – started by a group such as WWF (see page 46). You could even start your own petition.

Donate

Donating is not just about giving money, you can also give your time and energy. You can raise funds for conservation organizations by helping out in a street collection, collecting things for a jumble sale, taking part in a sponsored event, and so on. Bowling for Rhinos is a fundraising event to save rhino habitat in Africa and Asia. It runs sponsored bowling events across the USA to raise funds. You might raise money for general projects, or for specific things. For example, you can sponsor a particular rhino, rhino **warden** or rhino vet through groups such as SOS Rhino (see page 46).

This London Marathon runner is raising money for rhino conservation.

Glossary

Afrikaner   descendant of 17th century Dutch settlers in southern Africa

aid   money or other help given for people or animals in need

bacteria   tiny living things that rapidly increase in numbers in the right conditions

breed   process of having young, from finding another animal to mate with to rearing young

browser   animal that feeds largely on woody shrubs and trees

bull   male mammal, especially ungulates such as black rhino

bushveld   type of southern African habitat with large shrubs, such as acacia, and little grass

campaign   organized activity to bring about change

clan   community of animals, often related, such as black rhino

classify   group according to similarities such as shared traits

conservation   type of work people do to protect wildlife and the natural habitats of the world

cow   female mammal, especially ungulates such as black rhinos

customs   government department that controllings import and export of goods

ecosystem   community of organisms and their habitat

endangered   when a species has so few members it is in danger of dying out

extinct   when a species has died out and no longer exists

family   classification grouping. It usually includes several species.

genes   chemical codes that determine how things are and what they look like

habitat   place in the natural world where a particular organism lives

home range   area within a habitat in which an animal usually lives

inbreeding   when animals that are closely related breed and the population becomes weaker because they have very similar genes

jambiya   ceremonial dagger popular in Yemen and several other Middle Eastern countries

mammal   warm-blooded animal with hair that can feed its young with milk from its body

mate   when male animals fertilize eggs of female with their sperm

midden   communal dung pile

mineral   chemical needed by, but not made by, living things, such as calcium

mudwallow   pool where animals plaster mud on their skin to help them cool down

non-governmental organization (NGO)   group that raises money for conservation from donations by the public or businesses

parasite   living thing, such as a flea, that takes all it needs to live – nutrients and protection – from another living thing

poaching   illegal, usually secretive, hunting

predator   animal that hunts and eats other animals

prey   animal that is hunted and eaten by another animal

refugee   person who moves to another place to escape danger

sanctuary   type of protected area to safeguard endangered wildlife

smuggle   transport concealed goods illegally

species   type of animal that cannot breed successfully with any other type

spoor   footprints

subspecies   grouping of similar living things within a species

succulent   fleshy and containing water

territory   particular area an animal claims and defends as its own

tickbird   type of bird that feeds mostly on parasites living on the skin of large mammals such as black rhinos

tranquilizer   drug used to temporarily put an animal to sleep

translocation   moving an animal to a new place to live

ungulate   mammal with hooves

volunteer   person who works for no payment

warden   person paid to guard a particular area such as a reserve

weaned   when a young mammal has stopped suckling from its mother

Websites

WWF

www.panda.org

The WWF website contains information about the **Species** Programme it runs for the black rhino, including specific projects it is involved in.

Bowling for Rhinos

bfr.aazk.org

Bowling for Rhinos was set up by AAZK (American Association of Zoo Keepers) to help save rhinos and their **habitats**.

International Rhino Foundation

www.rhinos-irf.org

The International Rhino Foundation (IRF) is dedicated to the **conservation** of black, white, Sumatran, Javan and Indian rhinos.

Black Rhino Foundation

www.sosrhino.org

The Black Rhino Foundation is building awareness of the plight of the rhino and generating funding through concerts held around the world.

African Wildlife Foundation

www.awf.org

The African Wildlife Foundation has been working with the people of Africa since 1961, to protect their natural resources. Most of AWF's staff are in Africa, working with park managers and communities to protect wildlife and wilderness areas.

Rhino ARK

www.rhinoark.org/index.htm

Rhino ARK is committed to building a fence around the Aberdare Forest. Their website gives information about fundraising and also a plan to make posts out of recycled plastic.

IUCN
www.iucn.org
IUCN is the World Conservation Union. It offers specialist conservation advice and expertise about the world's rare animals and plants. Pachyderm, a journal dedicated to rhino and elephant conservation, can be viewed online at *iucn.org/themes/ssc/sgs/afesg/pachy/index.html*

Traffic
www.traffic.org
IUCN and WWF jointly run TRAFFIC, an organization that controls and monitors trade in rare organisms.

The David Sheldrick Trust
www.sheldrickwildlifetrust.org/html/rhino_conservation.html
The David Sheldrick Trust helps conserve rhinos in Kenya. The site includes information about rhino orphans and captive care.

The Sebakwe Black Rhino Trust
www.blackrhino.org/index.html
Focuses on saving Zimbabwe's black rhinos from extinction.

Books

Natural World: Black Rhino, Malcolm Penny (Hodder Children's Books, 2001)

Rhino: From the Brink of Extinction, Anna Merz (Collins, 1991)

Rhino Road: The Black and White Rhinos of Africa, Martin Booth (Constable, 1992)

Index

Titles in the *Animals Under Threat* series include:

Hardback   0 431 18892 0

Hardback   0 431 18888 2

Hardback   0 431 18889 0

Hardback   0 431 18893 9

Hardback   0 431 18890 4

Hardback   0 431 18891 2

Find out about the other titles in this series on our website www.heinemann.co.uk/library